Sundogs
& angels

ISBN: 978-0-9977343-2-4

Dedication: James 'Uncle Jim' Lafazia III
and Hershey,

You will never be forgotten.

CONTENTS

1   WIDE AWAKE
2   THE BRIDGE
3   SECOND HAND
5   LATE AUTUMN
6   QUIET
7   CLOVERS & KEEPSAKES
8   TO SIMPLY BE THERE
9   LONESOME SIMILARITIES
11 THE BEAUTIFUL NOW
12 CLOSE TO A MIRACLE
13 GLITTERING WONDER
16 SHADOW OF DOUBT
17 REST WELL, DEAR HEART
19 EDGE OF THE CRESCENT MOON
22 PAINTING IN THE DARK
24 NORMALCY
25 WISE SOUL
27 NONE CAN HAVE
29 CARRIED AWAY
30 ON A BRIDGE IN PONT NEUF
32 THE LAUGHING DOG
34 SILVER LINED TIGHT ROPE
37 LACK-LUSTER
39 MAD LAUGHTER
40 CHANCE TO BE
41 IN SEARCH OF SOMETHING
42 THOUGHTFUL
44 MIRRORS OF LIGHT

45 CASCADE OF COLOURS
46 UNPREDICTABLE TRUTH
48 ETCH YOUR NAME
49 APRIL SHOWERS
50 SAVING DAYLIGHT
53 RESEMBLES NEVERLAND
55 PEOPLE PATTERNS
56 A SHOT TOWARDS THE HORIZON
58 USELESS GLOOM
59 AS LIGHTLY AS AIR
61 DOGS & ANGELS
63 BLACK SUEDE
67 AGRO DOLCE
68 ELSEWHERE
70 SUMMER RAIN
71 INDEED DIFFERENT
73 FRAGILE
75 SUNDAY HOURS
77 SECRETS
79 PERFECT MOMENT
81 BLACKBIRD
84 SOMETHING IN COMMON
85 A CHANGED SEASON
86 TRICKLE
87 WILDFLOWER
89 THE MUSIC SHE PLAYED
90 THE SUN SKIPPED
91 WITHOUT AN AUDIENCE
93 HOW IT GOES
95 WHERE ANGELS DWELL
96 ACKNOWLEGE BEAUTY
97 RELAX
98 ART

99   STRIVING TO FEEL
100   BEAUTIFUL & PECULIAR THINGS
101   HEARTSET
103   EVER BLOOM
104   GOOD FINDINGS
106   BLOOMING FLOWERS
107   ANGEL EYES
109   WEIGHTLESS MELODY
111   WHERE A GARDEN ONCE WAS
113   THIN AIR
115   FASHIONABLY LATE
116   GALLERY
117   INSIGHT
118   SILENCE
119   A RESCUE IN STEADY RAIN
122   SULKING SHADOWS
123   FIREFLIES
125   TO ALWAYS BE
126   DAWN
128   HOW GRAND YOU ARE
129   LOST TREASURE
131   FIND IT ALL
133   EPIPHANY
135   PASSION
137   THE SKY
138   CARVED INTO THE HEART

Wake them from the nightmares.
She told me.

As the dog growled in his sleep
his paws move and fidget in an
effort to escape a bad dream.

She called his name

ever so gently.

As he woke

his tail began to wag.

*You have to wake them from the
nightmares.* She told me.

She had such a way of doing that.

It takes only

a touch of wonder

and we may revive the world.

Wide Awake

I had to know

her dreams,

carry each

with my own.

Even if nothing appeared

as we dreamt....

I knew this one

to be true.

I would not change a damn thing.

Wide awake

and still

we dream.

1

The Bridge

The Irony is life

is not always kind.

For the most part,

good people are.

Good people are delicate

as dancing light.

They illuminate.

They lead us to the bridge

over the darkened void

of false truths,

false love,

the silver lined lies.

Second Hand

We all start somewhere.

As long as we learn to think

for ourselves, we'll get through.

Many ideas

make an individual.

Most of these

are second hand.

After all, it must take

a lifetime to understand

how a variety of

madness

and reason

can create

something

solid enough

to live by.

Late Autumn

The morning light

of an Indian summer

glistened through the window

just before the leaves turned,

in this New England Fall.

This was the way we loved,

like late Autumn.

As the earth and her seasons

began to change,

somehow, we kept the cold away.

Quiet

You find yourself

quietly

in a quiet place without name,

where the slow air drifts.

As the glint and glow of

golden things

lend their light,

take notice.

Clovers & Keepsakes

Read a fair amount,

use clovers as bookmarks.

I am yet to find one

with four leaves.

Luck tends to run out,

so carry a keepsake

deep in the heart.

It bleeds into everything.

Nothing is absolute,

Most of life happens

at a moment's notice.

That is the thing

about a moment,

the ability

to simply be there.

Lonesome Similarities

We are going

through this solitude

in all kinds of ways.

With all we have made,

thoughts

of old days,

old friends

come about in more or less

the same old way.

What makes the difference

is when they arrive all at once,

we have no idea

what to make of it.

The Beautiful Now

Now is a good place to start

for those who care

to treat tomorrow

as though it is not.

You hold on to the day

say *look! ..... It is here –*

The beginning

of the beautiful now !

Close To A Miracle

The truth is nobody will offer you

anything besides good company

whilst you are together.

Though, some say

beautiful things

burn

very bright,

burn out

– turn to dust in our hands.

Yet, sometimes,

they stay alight,

growing old

and wise,

close to

some kind

of miracle.

Glittering Wonder

You always knew how to dream.

There must be more

to dreams, after all.

Mine often scatter in the early sun.

I am left with only a few

pictures in the mind.

Yet they resemble what is

endless and possible.

And if you have one dream,

just a single dream glittering so

wonderfully to stick with you

throughout,

that must mean

something special.

Shadow Of Doubt

When you left I felt it.

 It followed me

 in the shape of a shadow where

my own doubts appeared.

Like a fool, I began to feel sorry

for that - for myself

and it did not make sense..

Then I thought,

this is a dangerous habit.

Still, I doubt I will hear from you.

You are going after big things,

important things, you said.

I have no doubt you'll get there.

Rest Well, Dear Heart

Rest well, dear heart.

Rest well along the way,

have care and courage

when you speak,

and listen twice

for every word said.

Ease the mind by simple means,

enjoy good food.

Clear dark images from your

thinking,

they tire you

and make you sick.

A good drink, a meal

and a night's sleep will fix

a tired body

but fatigue of the heart and mind

can kill.

Edge Of The Crescent Moon

I get angry at things.

It has been easy to cry lately,

She said.

There is this hole in me.

A dark hole and I want to scream.

Tears fall, sometimes, I'm not

even sad.

It feels like I'm under still water.

Is this how people go mad?

You know, you cannot trust

anyone

without having seen their temper,

that goes for yourself, too.

I thought.

Everyone must go a little crazy

or they would lose it for good.

I know that place.

It is a deep well.

I told her.

You can sit

on the edge of

the crescent moon

and fish for things

very far down inside,

things that make all people alike.

But I do not like to swim in there.

I said

Me neither, she replied,

Then she smirked, like sunshine.

That grew gradual into laughter

and lightened the room,

something had moved

in her and I.

Painting In The Dark

You can't paint in the dark, I said

The bedroom light flickered,

the wires frayed and exposed.

It was broken.

She wanted to put up a picture.

So we painted anyway

- the walls, the ceiling –

I edged the baseboards and

crown moulding,

The light flickered above us.

This'll strengthen our minds, she

said,

as I laughed,

and we painted.

We didn't notice the broken light

above us for a while.

Afterward, I repaired the light.

The next day, she put up a picture

of Paris

with the Eiffel Tower

in black and white.

Normalcy

We will remain childish.

We tend to trade this

for a sense of mundane normalcy.

Most want for only a normal life.

We aren't quite sure what that is.

The remarkable things called

normal.

We may delve in,

reach a place that sparkles rough,

where what is made

of magic

does not die.

Wise Soul

I met a wise soul once.

We'll meet many

throughout our lives.

Sometimes, we'll get lucky,

and they stick around for the ride.

Some teach

and remind us

why we have come.

An old dog.

taught me more about life and it's

spirit than any school or religion

ever could.

He taught patience,

and that life has teeth,

and to approach it with respect

and trust.

It is not to be coddled, or

neglected.

It is to love, and believe that there

is something unspoken that binds

us.

Life will show its teeth.

Sometimes, it will bite,

and sometimes,

it'll give you a gentle nudge,

curl up at your feet,

and keep watch while you sleep.

None Can Have

When something becomes stale,

It is because certain things require

your life.

And you are not going to give

such a precious gift to any old

something.

You seek a passion that blooms

within bone

- to breathe the wildest air,

to walk the wild wood,

to hear the finest laughter

the way the city shines

in the evening rain,

Brick-top buldings over glistening

cobblestone streets,

as a star full night

drapes the rolling sea.

You must take your now,

Forgive your yesterdays

and enjoy all of your tomorrows.

Carried Away

Anyone may begin again,

you know?

It didn't matter who you were

or how you carried yourself.

You could start fresh,

all bright and new.

Most people do it.

Yet, all that truly changes

is the way you carry your heart.

A Bridge In Pont Neuf

After a few years,

They cut the love locks

from the famous bridges

in the city of Paris.

On the Quai de la Tournelle,

an old faded green Citroen is

parked by the Seine.

Houses line a path time hardly

touched.

To capture an eternal youth,

we need only a second,

a kiss on a day in September,

a photograph

on a bridge in Pont Neuf.

The Laughing Dog

This may only be a wishful

thought.

Pretend with me for a moment.

What if this isn't it and it is not

so complicated,

and one beautiful fine day,

we'll wake to each other as I say

my, my, what a terrible dream. I

lost you to something called

death. Everyone lost to it and we

had to be brave to live that way till

it came for us."

You'll smile and say *Really?*

Me too, but come on now,

how silly.

The laughing dog will jump

on the bed again.

We will get up,

happy and together?

Till that wishful then,

the end of something will lead

back to the beginning,

all the places we once stood and

every path we ever took.

I will miss and never forget you

and that beloved laughing dog.

Silver Lined Tight Rope

You cannot truly know

of life till you have

let go

of love for its own good.

Left to hope you'll

have it again

somewhere we needn't suffer.

We will walk along the silver

lining.

Thinking strange

how this goes.

One thing

turns to the next.

Happiness is our choice,

I have heard some say,

but that becomes

hard once loss turns to pain,

sorrow to despair

to doubt

to pity.

Sadness spills out and down

upon others.

It doesn't take too much

to be happy

till it requires every fucking thing.

But to recognize what is real

in a world of make believe,

we need the very things that scar

and tear

to save us

after all.

Lack- Luster

Some are very clever,

the way they attempt

to frighten and trouble,

to make these rotten things yours.

As a terrible shiver runs down

the spine,

remember,

fear is an antique.

Worry is only a tired thought.

Hate is always

an easy out.

Remember those who shine

over the lack-luster things

which aim to defeat us.

Mad Laughter

Because otherwise I may

weep endlessly

or break out in mad laughter

at the fact this is reality.

Certain thoughts lead

to a restless mind

stumbling here and there.

I get a strange hollow feeling

between the gut and the heart.

Perhaps, the soul

is kept there

and does not like to be prodded.

Chance To Be

Often, you do not realize

till much later.

Painful things go deep and

do not bleed

till you begin to patch up.

Then you understand

had the well-lighted road

been travelled,

you would have not had a chance

to be any better.

In Search Of Something

Everywhere is alive

with stories and secrets.

The sound of the city reminds us

life goes on.

Sirens say things could always be

worse.

When in search of something

to wish upon,

the trick is to get away

once in a while.

As shooting stars get lost

in the city lights.

Thoughtful

Stay thoughtful.

Considerate.

We never know what might

happen.

Some days you'll want

to tell the world to piss off,

by all means, shout it clear.

Drive toward the sun.

Laugh as the city shrinks in the

rearview as the day becomes

ours.

And in tired times - in need of a

restful moment to shake the worst

off,

go easy

and know this day too

is ours.

Mirrors Of Light

There is all sorts

of nonsense in this world.

People become consumed by

their own thoughts

their own beliefs

even their own identities.

Maybe the true self

is beneath all that

driving our senses crazy

in the most beautiful way.

The way water mirrors light.

Cascade Of Colors

To take my days full with passion

to last the night through morning,

mad for all I love and able

to never look back,

unless for the hand

of those I care for;

to pull them forward.

Often. I forget the rules.

Rules on how to do things,

how to feel,

love,

or be someone,

I want to bend them till they snap

and shatter into a glorious

cascade of colors.

I want the beautiful things,

the truly good and just and moral,

and those brave enough to stand

without judgment.

Let me take any shred of

frustration and doubt and burn it,

and use the fire to warm you

and bring to light everything

we need to just be.

Unpredictable Truth

In our darkest times,

when the abyss stares into us,

a small speck of our own light

may become the roaring sun.

As there is a strength and

resilience you cannot read of

or watch on any screen.

It is intangible.

It is a place within you,

Though unpredictable

and anything but pretty,

this place is found in each of us,

pouring truth as it appears.

Etch Your Name

So long as I am here I always think

of you,

You need not worry.

I will etch your name in a starlit

night.

When the stars do not show

themselves,

I will write it myself with a full hard

stare.

And afterward, if I do it just right

something may stay

for others to find.

April Showers

In 1988 the rain fell from April to

May.

I spent a few nights looking down

at the clouds.

Whether coming or going, aurora

eyes left tears.

And so you are a living poem,

and I a rag and bone man,

attempt to scavenge the words

you bring.

Those April showers turned to

diamonds.

I am still here watching them

dance on your skin.

I remember when I asked where I

fit in this world,

you said in your arms.

We laughed about that

as we learned to

long ago.

Saving Daylight

You must steal an hour to save

daylight.

The clock on the mantel said

1:59 am

in dashed digital numbers

then 3am and

2 o' clock vanished.

Do the stars notice?

They only shimmer steadfast, and

remain largely indifferent.

We once had the keys to time,

to an old grandfather clock.

The key fit in the clock face and
turned the arrowed hands
backward in circles past the
roman numerals.

You would hear the cogs tick
along inside where a little door
opened to the inner workings of
time.

I thought how strangely
marvelous and grand it was as I
watched my father steal an hour
to save daylight.

Resembles Neverland

Take me to a place that

resembles Neverland.

where all is fantastic and

make believe,

in this beautiful place

full of beaches and lagoons,

where you meet good friends

and eat good food

and take off on adventures

to journey as long or as short as

you wished,

so long as you had fun.

What went on or happened was

no matter,

at day's end, everything would be

splendid

and good and all right,

because there would always be

somewhere that never grew old.

People Patterns

You shouldn't ignore them,

they say

 – the patterns in people.

Though, sometimes we see

patterns

where there are none.

That's the problem with a pattern

–

to notice when it is only a trick of

the eye

and not to live by such things.

A Shot Towards The Horizon

Life is the art

of pulling yourself through.

I took a shot in the dark.

It fizzled and lit the corner of the

room before it faded.

Some figure out what to do by

crossing off the things

you shouldn't.

I suppose I'd keep it alight.

I had to. No one else would.

Today, I may be a Crow, or a

humble Swallow.

I'd whirl thousands of feet in the

air on days like this.

I'd never lose sight of the horizon.

Useless Gloom

The thing is

no one will come to save you –

pull you from

an awful

useless gloom

and make everything better.

You have to do it

and you will

– when no one else is around

because it is

meant only for you

to overcome.

As Lightly As Air

We feel the weight of life's

decisions

in our hands

through to the shoulders -

we carry it.

We strive, fail – often miserably.

Then, we pick up

and have another go

till it feels natural.

We move

light-footed,

ever so lightly.

We begin to free

from which no longer fits.

Dogs And Angels

It was late February.

An evening she gathered

her scattered heart

and wiped away bad memories

that made mascara run.

And when she opened that door

the room fell

silent.

A song played

somewhere,

only dogs and

angels heard it.

Right then,

I had to know her name.

Black Suede

Paint the doors black suede,

because nothing quite buried

your soul

and you're digging in.

They come for light, blindly.

You glimmer and appear

alongside it all,

in flow,

from that place you keep clean,

clear and unspoiled.

I have loved you sincerely.

Cost Of Landing

We reached the edge,

and it was time to

take a leap

of faith.

Words have their way.

A glimpse

into the future.

A bird taking flight

that will never

pay the cost

of landing.

Reaching

everything.

Everything that is,

and all that could be.

If only we take off

on time

under her patient wing.

To glide forever,

disappearing

when need be,

Knowing nothing

ever ends.

It all goes on

with, or

without us,

and that

is what makes

a moment,

worth living.

Agro Dolce

Anthony bourdain explained

Agro Dolce in comparison to

a Japanese flower eaten after

a meal, as he sat with a sushi

master.

That's Italian - agro dolce,

sweet, spicy, sweet, spicy,

and then something bitter

at the end

to remind you of the sadness.

That sentence sort of defined life

for me.

Elsewhere

I was drawn to you.

We were always after what wasn't

quite here.

We would drive all night to

the middle of nowhere –

The engine hummed, the wind

whistled alongside.

The road had a sound

that brought us closer.

White lines slipped into blacktop.

We parked the car and put the

radio on.

You turned up the volume.

The backlight on the dial shines.

 The silence filled with

rock and roll.

Summer Rain

As the fog rolled in,

in spite of me,

soft summer rain

suspended in the sky,

As the birds danced

at the opportunity for a

spontaneous

rain bath,

we decided to stay awhile.

Indeed Different

You give

and give and give

till you are adrift,

and there

You will stay

if you are not careful.

The feelings arrive in waves -

pressure in places

no one will notice,

a high pitch in your ear,

a twitch of the brow

till you breathe fully,

deep and clear

and realize you are indeed

different

and thank goodness for that.

Fragile

It's reckless and beautiful,

and love often is careless.

Don't let it

make your heart heavy.

Only the reckless

can love like you,

and only the beautiful

have such strength.

But the way you carry

your fragile heart

on your sleeve,

I just know,

such fragile things often break

Sunday Hours

I love you like I love the stars,

you said.

But they burnt out in the night.

The morning shone with a

thousand birds over the hazy sea.

It is just not quite the way it was.

I suppose that's the story of life.

I watch the days change,

went from midnight to midday,

and besides the fading night,

I felt more or less a sameness.

But it is Monday now.

I am stuck on Sunday hours.

Secrets

Words complicate everything,

and the eyes often only tell you

what you want to know.

True secrets are like that

you have to really

know a person to see

their secrets.

to know what they hide,

what they bury.

Often so deep

they cannot find it them self.

You have to have mapped

more than the stars within them.

even a gut feeling that

slowly sinks into a bitter truth

can be misleading.

We often break

our own hearts

with our

own minds,

and that is

our own madness.

Perfect Moment

It takes only a second,

a perfect moment.

You want something

to last.

You rush after it, and plan for it,

wait for days, months, years,

and it is strange that the minutes

that lead to them

feel longest,

but I will tell you this – the magic

of the things you remember most

will be in between.

It'll be between people and

places and not things at all.

Something sudden that'll find you

as you walk down a quiet street,

in an almost endless second after

a good-bye.

You decide

you cannot have any part of life

unless it is lived

like this.

Blackbird

I sat down

to rest on warm grass;

a hot day

in late spring.

A day where the breeze

complements the sun,

working together in unison.

As the old oak tree

greets the sky

with a gentle wave.

I watch a blackbird

rest on a powerline,

next to the old brick chimney,

I should probably inspect for

leaks.

Somehow, nature will always

find a way in,

no matter how skilled the labour.

She has time on her side,

and skills no man can master.

I watch the blackbird

make himself at home.

As if those lines

had been put there just for him.

I wonder if he understands

the power beneath him,

how it lights the darkness,

helps shelter souls

and warm cold bones.

I wonder if I'm a blackbird.

You are alive

with all this feeling

darting about,

highest highs, lowest lows

- ups, downs

and in betweens

have a strange something

in common.

A Changed Season

Perhaps,

you will not look at me that way

again.

We are changed now.

Mistakes made.

Moments gone, passed, missed.

How time rushes like melting ice.

The season is cold here.

Trickle

In the trickle of time,

before you know it,

a life has been poured at your

feet, for better or worse you are

here amongst this,

in life's midst.

And it is the names you carve

on the heart.

Some things hold enough

to last longer than us,

though we are unable to tell why.

It is in the seconds none see, for

the stories and the songs

within each of us.

Wildflower

She lost sleep.

Worried her dreams may not

remember her name.

She stays up all night,

Tossing and turning.

She shuts people out.

And sometimes, that's a good

thing.

She would listen to the birds.

They always had something good

to say. It wasn't complicated and

she didn't need to make sense of

it all.

They left wildflowers blooming in

her heart.

That would remind her

of something more.

The Music She Played

I decided. I ought to be there.

I need her.

The music she played.

The books she read.

Those nights, she'd fall asleep

with a book page down,

open on the bed.

I would turn the music down,

Softly

place the open book

on the nightstand with a

wilted flower on the page.

The Sun Skipped

I loved the way your laughter

set the world alight with color.

It was like the sun skipped

as it split the clouds.

Pure and golden light hung gently

over the trees as if to say I love

you.

Without a word the day spoke

of all

we felt.

Without An Audience

Get comfortable in your skin.

There is solace

when you are alone.

You will meet yourself.

As most of us are patchworks of

what we admire.

People pretend to be people

then loneliness dawns slowly

when there is no longer an

audience.

Don't be one of them

You must know yourself so well

to not become someone else.

How It Goes

It is hard how it goes.

In some moments,

we turn back into lost children

in search of all the things we once

touched, in all the places we once

stood and we try not to forget.

That's the thing about endings.

They lead back to the beginning.

They bring the real person out to

feel and question more than

ordinary things.

It always hurts

when we are led

to where love once was.

Where Angels Dwell

Angels dwell here

with tails

that thump the ground

and big eyes

that understand.

Sometimes,

The best thing

To do

Is acknowledge

What is beautiful.

Relax

Why must the mind read

Into what does not matter,

subtle little things

burrow under the skin

and make you regret, slipped

between words and glances

and crossed arms and shifting

feet, Uncertain what to do

with themselves?

The awkward things that make up

doubt are rarely unique.

Try to relax.

You are not the only one

who feels this much.

Art

We all have it.

A small piece of

a blackened heart.

Bitter, unforgiving,

a merciless bastard.

Finding it before it kills you

is the gift.

Understanding it is the power.

Letting it heal is the love.

And cutting it out

while it is still beating

this is the art.

Striving To Feel

Maybe more than anything else,

It is not about striving to feel

a particular way constantly.

Maybe, it is but to simply be there

in all things with all you feel.

Perhaps in this way,

you may take the time

to not be so hard on yourself.

Beautiful And Peculiar Things

In the way you looked at me,

in the way you smiled.

The way a quiet day together

brought music

into the background.

I understood

how love is made

quietly

from beautiful and peculiar things.

Heartset

You're pacing again, said the
heart.

Winding through thought, replied
the mind.
In still pictures of pretty places?
The mind asked.

Yes replied the heart.
Many places all at once.

I don't know how you do it.
I cannot stay in one place for long,
the mind began to explain,

When I set myself on certain

things others often get in the

way....

Don't think about it so much.

Be still and follow me, the heart

said.

You still remember how to put

me back together if I ever am

to break, don't you?

Always, replied the mind

then *Let me set our course,* the

heart said.

I'll find us somewhere safe.

Ever Bloom

Every thought

is in the shape of you…

How you look forward

with that warm glow of grace

which lightened me.

Through a path of brambles,

under an oak terrace

of Spanish moss,

some shining thing calls out

All the world is yours

for a moment at least.

The things that make you

wonderful do not change.

I see you ever bloom.

Good Findings

Finding the good

depends

on one's thinking.

We go through this alone yet

together.

We look into a mirror

reflecting us

In others.

While there may be

Hard times

Dissatisfaction

Disappointment

Certain promises made

- Some broken

-    Some kept.

There will also be joy

and friendship

- the wonder of the new

- the comfort of the old.

The good always becomes

part of you.

Rest not

On a promise,

But Like the scent

Of spring,

Rise

From the frost

With a mouthful

Of blooming flowers.

Angel Eyes

Angels were once described as

winged creatures

with a thousand eyes.

No one could look at them

without losing their mind.

The Angel's wing held a thousand

weeping eyes.

They must see into what is

ancient and timeless.

 And once you realize you are

not quite like any other,

you may think you are more alone

than ever before.

Hardly anyone thinks anymore,

seeking only to be reassured.

And when they see an Angel,

like you,

in its truest form,

they attempt to butcher it.

Weightless Melody

I am content

to look for the good

to keep me company.

As I hum old songs

I have not heard

in years.

Funny, how they stay

with you

unnoticed

how the good things

may be

as weightless

as an old melody.

Where A Garden Once Was

There was something here once.

You still felt it.

Moments linger in energy and

atmosphere.

I learned as I opened the door.

I looked out at a rooftop where a

garden once was.

Now the roof leaks where it once

held perennial flowers,

herbs, heather, berries and

alliums.

I felt I was late

yet something special was there -

something that leads

to ghost stories

and legends.

Thin Air

Tomorrows turn into yesterdays.

The same days felt

as though they'd last

forever.

And then they reached the end

though none of us realized

till the weeks became distant.

Yesterday may as well

have been

months ago.

That day with you is clearer than

this minute that just went by.

It is quarter past five now

wasn't it just four o clock?

perhaps I am daydreaming again.

How thoughts of

distant days gone by

appear

Like Snowdrop flowers in

February,

out of the cold thin air.

.

Fashionably Late

You will have time

once you spend it wisely.

But please don't be late....not you...

You will miss too much.

Though some may stay

through it all.

Some cannot,

And you do not know

once time is up.

Because the irony of time

is how you spend it.

Gallery

I want to be inside you,

inside your mind,

in the dark corners

with all of your cobwebs.

I want to see all the hidden

pieces,

Beautifully lost in your gallery,

in a puzzle I will never try to solve,

for the possibility to stay.

Completely covered

in your canvas.

With every brushstroke

they never took the time

to see.

Sometimes, sight has nothing

to do with our eyes.

Silence

She sits in

silence.

Silence

that hides

a thousand

screams

behind a

broken smile

and shattered

eyes

staring at

a world

that can

only see

its own

reflection.

A Rescue in Steady Rain

In a secret garden in May, we
watched the rain with a rescue
dog.

The sky filled with dark swirling
clouds then lightning,
seconds later thunder roared.
I counted
one.....two.....three....
A storm was closing in.

My wife told me of her dream
last night,
of walking a path
of wilted sunflowers.
They grew vibrant and fresh as
she walked towards a temple,
towards
a holy man

in maroon red robes,
He was sat, she said, on a tall
throne.

He looked down at her
with a serious look
and took a drink
from what appeared
to be a bottle of beer.

 I opened the door, as she spoke
over roaring thunder,
The dog decided better not to
go outside.

A tornado siren howled in the
distance. The wind became fierce.
As rain fell sideways then
suddenly all was quiet.
The gods had touched the earth
three miles away.

Sulking Shadows

What we constantly fight

in the heart and mind

are not demons,

only sulking shadows

made up in the dark.

Thoughts made of the worst of
things,

melded with us and our
worrisome what ifs,

old fashioned anxieties and fears,

like a grafted monster.

These demons turn out to be
more akin

to a stack of old clothes on a chair
in a dark corner,

casting shadows on the wall,

in need of a little light.

Once you see clear,

you take a seat.

You realize you have just won

the most important fight there is.

Fireflies

I don't weep
for lovers.
They tend to break
their own hearts.

I found that place
to weep for others.

As two fireflies
flickered by,

they disappeared
into the stars.

I do not want for much,
 only a chance to be -
To be with you while you sleep
To hold you whilst you dream
To wake next to you each day
I want it always to be this way.

Dawn

She would rise before the sun.
As I treat the minutes like hours,
somehow dreaming in thirty
second intervals,

never the same dream which
always annoyed me,

like going to the movies only to
have the screen burnout halfway
through.

That has happened to me before.
They offer a refund.
It is not the same.

Dreams don't offer
any compensation for interruption.

It was dawn.

A time that should be reserved for
the birds,

as only they have the grace of
early mornings.

As I turn the corner the sun and I
would meet, with a quick
reminder there are gods at work.

Perhaps the ending of everything
makes anything bearable.

The mind is as grand or as small
as its focus.

Bear witness to how grand
you are

It is no small mistake you are here.

Lost Treasure

There's a feeling that will
pierce through
when your eyes feel full with tears
but there are none.

Only a heavy sigh weights you
against it all.

Rest here for a moment.
And in this moment,
delve into the many moments
that happily go on and on.

You still see them, hear them
– almost taste them.

But you have buried them
like a lost treasure

to be found where pointed
starlight drops out of a hollow
night.

Find It All

I need to find it all.
All the chaos
All the tranquility
All the madness
All the serenity
All the fight
All the peace
I need to find all of you,
and all of me.

I need your dreams
to find me while I sleep.
But I find I do not want
to close my eyes,
and allow this moment
to slip through my cracks.

I need to find your darkness.
To feel it surround me so I can
dream in your scent,

and I need your light to wake
the sky
so I may find it all again.

Epiphany

There is so much

To the world

The influence of

The people

The places

Their beauty

Their horror

Their joy

The sorrow

Is incomprehensible.

When the world began to eat

itself the loss of context

is what got under the skin.

How influence is subtle, words

and thoughts articulated well

and full of conviction,

once read in your mind's voice

often feel similar to a conclusion

of your own.

How easily we may kid ourselves.

To form an idea or identity from

another's influence as our own

thoughts are drowned.

Whereas some prefer a straight
line,

once we join the dots,

we are able to draw conclusions.

We deserve our own epiphanies.

Passion

We do not understand it.
All this passion
this burning passion
that leaves its mark
within us all.

It is too violent
to ignore.
searing
through bone,
spouting roses from our skulls.

a reminder
you are not alone,
not the only one
that glows red-hot
for something more.

For someone
to make us more,
and I, too,

need someone.

Someone like you
to tend to the fire.

When I stare too long at the sky,
I start to see the rain.
It is rain I cannot feel.
It is this rain that feels familiar,
and the sky will always
remember,
Those the world forgot.

Promise me.
We will never grow up,
not in our hearts.
Know that we can never die,
even if we must grow old.
Always remember this room
with shades of us,
the tick of a clock
drowned by our song.

. Forgive me,
I do not tread lightly.
I will not make a sound.

I will leave a mark
in places you
never knew were there.

Until you lay down your armor,
and find my name carved into
your heart

Other work:

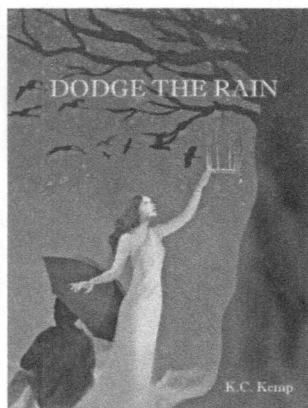

For excerpts and news about upcoming books
follow on Instagram: @k.c.kemp